THE boozy BLENDER

THE  boozy BLENDER

Bruce Weinstein & Mark Scarbrough

PHOTOGRAPHY BY EVAN SUNG

CLARKSON POTTER/PUBLISHERS
NEW YORK

Published in the United States by Clarkson Potter/
Publishers, an imprint of the Crown Publishing
Group, a division of Random House LLC,
a Penguin Random House Company, New York.
www.crownpublishing.com
www.clarksonpotter.com

CLARKSON POTTER is a trademark and
POTTER with colophon is a registered
trademark of Random House, LLC.

Library of Congress
Cataloging-in-Publication Data is
available upon request.

ISBN 978-0-8041-8670-4
eISBN 978-0-8041-8671-1

Printed in China

Book design by Ashley Tucker
Cover design by Jessie Bright
Cover photography by Evan Sung
Photography by Evan Sung

10 9 8 7 6 5 4 3 2 1

First Edition

contents

INTRODUCTION

IT'S SATURDAY AFTERNOON. The sun's just starting its long salaam to the west. You've worked in the yard all day and you want something icy-slushy, fruit-laced, and refreshing to help you kick back: a drink with hints of citrus, a bit of rum (to ease those sore muscles), and a smooth, rich texture. You reach for the blender.

Or it's Friday evening. A cold front has blown in; the temperature outside is headed below freezing. As logs crackle on the fire and the soft light begins to ease the tension of a long week, you want a treat, something creamy and a little decadent, with a touch of bourbon to ward off the chill. You're craving mellower flavors with fewer fruit notes and an earthier taste: a sophisticated sip for the kid inside. Once again, you pull out the blender.

Summer or winter, afternoon or evening, you want a frozen drink. And we've got your back. *The Boozy Blender* is our latest collection of cocktail delights: new flavor combinations, a few old favorites perfected for the modern kitchen, and lots of terrific ways to shave the edge off the day.

We're happy to be back in this game—it's been a long time since we've written about frozen drinks. Sure, we've been drinking them but we haven't published a frozen drink book in more than a decade. Wow, times have changed!

First off, there's a wider selection of just about everything involved in the process. There are more frozen fruit choices, better fresh berries, and a wider range of mixers on the market. Plus, the variety of fruit-based liqueurs and syrups is outrageous. Don't worry: We won't call for anything strange. No betel juice liqueur here! But we all now know that there's more to triple sec than the tongue burn from cheap alcohol. And we can all take advantage of the wider array of micro-batch vodkas and small-run rums to make our slushy potations extraordinary. There's no point in rotgut, even in a poolside drink.

Booze aside, twenty-first-century drink mavens now home-make just about every element of a cocktail. Frankly, we're thrilled because this time around, we, too, get to show off our recipes for falernum, dram syrup, and grenadine. Back in the '90s, friends called us "nuts" when we made these. Now, we're loping with the (well-lubricated) herd. You'll find our ingredient recipes throughout under the header DIY Excess.

However, we don't call for any flavored vodkas. We prefer the taste of fresh juice, rather than a vodka shortcut. As a general rule, we want more punch in every sip, not less. If we're going for a powerhouse hit, we'll use a raspberry or peach liqueur, a more intense note than a raspberry or peach vodka. A liqueur will also give the drink more body and a touch of sweetness without our having to add sugar.

Blenders have also improved overall since we last tackled this topic. As a general rule, they've got more powerful motors and stronger blade action, even if the models come in various levels of brawn. There are the standard kitchen blenders with better control and more stable canisters, the semiprofessional models with metal canisters that have long graced bars across the country, and the big behemoths, the power monsters that pack up to 4 horsepower under the hood and can blend frozen drinks in seconds (right after you've ground wheatberries into flour or bricks into quarry dust). Every drink in this book can be made in any of these blenders, provided (here's a caveat) that you watch the timings and have the hang of your machine.

Supercharged blenders will do the job in seconds, in less time than we recommend. Standard kitchen blenders will require a little more attention—like flicking the motor on and off, shaking the canister occasionally, and making sure to stop the machine if you need to rearrange the ingredients inside. After proper measuring, knowing your equipment is the second biggest part of perfecting a frozen drink.

Across the board, the blender canisters have also gotten larger. Thus, these recipes make *two* drinks *each*, not just one. In fact, if you have a blender canister larger than 56 ounces, you can double these recipes and make four drinks in one go. You can start your party with a single batch. Now there's a change worth celebrating.

Throughout this book, we've included some garnishing ideas for those of us who think looking good is a part of drinking good. We've also included some ways to take a concoction to the next level under the header "Like a Pro" (e.g., using an aged tequila, rather than a silver one). And we've called for specific glassware for a few drinks because the aesthetics of cocktails drive some of us writerly/foodie OCDs nuts. (Obviously that drink's going to taste the same, no matter the glass. So feel free to ignore our recs.) Finally, we've put together a collection of simple nibbles, snacks that go great with cocktails. None have a formal recipe—all are narrative ideas to make your party better.

Before we get to the drinks themselves, let's talk about the five most pressing concerns for success. Here's where the rubber meets the road—or the blender blades hit the ice.

the five things you need to know to make perfect frozen drinks

1 HOW TO USE A BLENDER Okay, let's dispense with the niceties. Plug it in. Keep the lid on (unless you're keen on repainting your kitchen). And don't operate it in the sink, tub, or pool. In fact, don't operate it *near* the sink, tub, or pool.

The machine does its blending with blades spinning inside a closed compartment. This may seem obvious, too—but it's amazing how many people stick a wooden spoon in there while the thing's whirring away. Do not do this under any circumstances. In fact, it's best to unplug the blender before reaching inside, period. And take care when you clean out the canister. The tipsy should not be around sharp blades. (A word to the wise should be sufficient.)

Incidentally, those blades wear out with time and ice. If you've used your blender a lot over a few years, or even if you've used it infrequently over the past decade, you should probably order new blades. Otherwise, making a drink stocked with ice will be as fun as trying to carve a turkey with a butter knife.

> **note:** You may find that ingredients do not blend as efficiently and quickly in older or less powerful models. To get past this sticking point, we recommend turning the machine off and shaking the canister gently, thereby rearranging the ingredients inside so every bit can reach the blades.

2 HOW TO MEASURE INGREDIENTS Get a jigger, that small, two-sided measuring device favored by bartenders across these United States. Generally, one side measures ½ or 1 U.S. fluid ounce and the other side measures 1 or 1½ U.S. fluid ounces.

If you insist on making frozen drinks with measuring spoons—and being laughed off your block—remember that

1 ounce = 2 tablespoons and (thus) ½ ounce = 1 tablespoon. Don't say we didn't warn you. The potted show little mercy to the unprofessional.

> **note:** As you measure these ingredients, keep in mind that while you can be a bit looser when measuring the base spirits—brandy, bourbon, vodka, rum, and tequila—you should be more exacting with fruit juices and concentrates. *And* you should be very exacting with fruit liqueurs, shrubs, bitters, and other flavorings. Another splash of vodka isn't going to kill a frozen drink. A little extra frozen lemonade concentrate and the thing might taste a bit off. But add twenty-five percent more vanilla-flavored liqueur, or triple sec, or ginger shrub, and your creation will be distinctly out of whack—and maybe the worst sin of all, undrinkable.

For accuracy, we recommend putting the ice or frozen fruit in first, before you start working with the jigger. Some blender mavens insist on adding ice last, claiming you get less ice melt if you add the cubes at the end. We believe they may have failed physics in high school. What are we talking about? One or two teaspoons of melt? Seriously? Put the cubes in first for a better consistency: slushier, creamier, with fewer crunchy chunks of ice. Yes, consistency is the hobgoblin of blender jockeys everywhere. But even if you prefer an icier drink, you'll get more uniform results if you follow our instructions.

Of course, all this ice advice is moot if you have one of those blenders on steroids, the ones that can powder an iPhone. It really doesn't matter what order you add the ingredients in those things. Just cover the canister before you turn it on.

3 **HOW TO GET THE RIGHT CONSISTENCY** Our preferences aside, this is a matter of practice rather than of rule because the final consistency of any frozen drink is a matter of taste. Some people like a grainier texture, thousands of little bits of ice that flick across the tongue in a single gulp. These

types should stop the blender quickly, just as a whirlpool starts to form in the center of the drink. Others prefer a creamier, smoother, more uniform consistency, similar to a slushy drink from a convenience store. These types should let that whirlpool grow and deepen to make sure every speck has plunged at least once to the blades.

It's up to you to play with your blender and figure out the right ratio of power to timing. We've given you visual cues throughout, but you should stop and sample the drinks as you make the first few. Soon enough, you'll know how to eyeball it. And practice was never so much fun.

4 HOW TO STOP SEPARATION Let's admit it right up front: Without the addition of corn syrup or chemical emulsifiers, almost all frozen drinks will eventually separate, the liquids on the bottom and the airy, lighter fruit puree on top—some, within a minute, others, over ten.

Sometimes we can solve the problem with natural thickeners like the chewy bulk in bananas or the thick pulp in berries. But without these (and even with them in some cases), we must combat separation with very cold ingredients. Keep the ice cubes in the freezer until you're ready to blend, not in a bowl next to the blender. The softer the ice, the quicker the drink will separate in the glass. And keep all fruit juices, concentrates, and nectars as cold as possible. Room temperature juice will quickly melt that slushy consistency.

All preventative measures aside, plan on serving these drinks with swizzle sticks. God created them to keep frozen drinks mixed. Swirl as you sip.

> note: We use swizzle sticks for private messages, a sort of social gathering semaphore for the long-married. One of us quietly taps a stick on a glass rim to tell the other that he's in the process of making a horrid gaffe. *Um, that's her mother-in-law you're talking to*

right now! Leaving a swizzle stick beside an empty glass means *Get me out of here*; leaving it in the glass means *I'm okay to stay*. See, very helpful.

5 **A SOLID DEFENSE AGAINST BRAIN FREEZE** Or as it's more commonly known, *sphenopalatine ganglioneuralgia.* Here's the problem: You're hot and you're eating ground ice. Some of your major cranial nerves run through your mouth. Sooner or later, they're going to feel the freeze—and shoot the cold right up toward your brain. To palliate the pain, you need to warm up your soft palate (the tender, concave depression at the back of the roof of your mouth). First, jam your tongue against your soft palate, thereby gently warming it. Next, tilt your head back to reduce the blood flow slightly. Finally, breathe in so warm air runs across your soft palate, gently bringing it back to proper temperature. Or, alternatively, just quit drinking for a minute.

Now that we've got the basics covered, we can get down to the nuts and bolts of frozen drinks. Next up, ten tips to get you going.

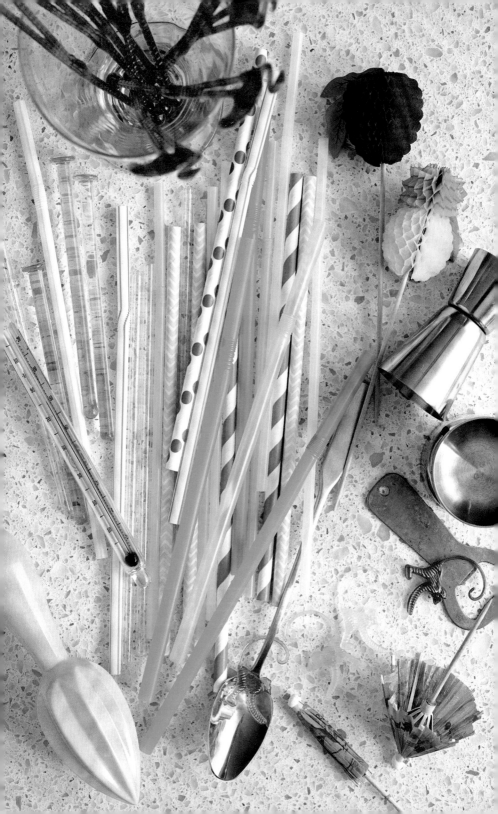

ten finesse points for frozen drinks

1 SMALL ICE CUBES Face it: Big honkers will not blend evenly or easily without a turbo machine. Every drink in this book was tested and retested with those smallish, half-moon ice cubes that almost every automatic built-in icemaker produces. If you're using ice cubes from trays, you'll need to put them in a small bag and whack them a couple of times with a hammer. If you buy ice, you'll need to do the same with the bigger bag to chip up what's inside. Don't think you can solve the problem by buying shaved or chipped ice; these will result in watery drinks, no one's idea of success.

> **note:** For optimal results, we've given you the weight of average ice cubes for each recipe. This may seem ridiculously fussy, but we want to make sure you know just what we mean by our measurements. Yes, you can scoop the ice up by the cupful; but weighing it will make better drinks—and win you major points with the foodies.

2 SILVER LIQUOR It's what we call the nonaged stuff: silver tequila, silver rum. Some brands (and cocktail writers) call it "white" liquor. In any event, we mean the clear liquid, not the brown. By the way, we never call for gold rum. In most cases, gold rum is actually silver rum with food coloring. You can, of course, substitute it for any silver rum used in the book—with the understanding that there may be a slight color shift in the resulting drink.

3 TYPES OF RUM Beyond silver rum, we call for two other kinds. First, there's aged rum—in other words, aged-in-oak rum. You needn't buy an expensive sipping rum, but you'll want a sturdy, solid offering, something with woody and molasses notes. Second, there's spiced rum, a mix of rum and various warm spices (like cinnamon). It's available in all sorts of bottlings, some ridiculously sweet, others with bitter and herbaceous overtones. Or make your own (see page 110).

4 **JUICE VERSUS NECTAR** A fruit juice is just that: the squeezed, extracted liquid from a fruit or berry, sometimes with the pulp intact and sometimes not. (In a blender drink, it won't much matter except that citrus pulp will give the drink a slightly spongy texture.) A nectar, by contrast, is fruit juice with sweeteners (and sometimes thickeners) added. Don't confuse the two, and make sure to use the one called for.

5 **FRUIT SYRUPS** These are made from concentrated, boiled-down, or otherwise reduced fruit juices, sometimes sweetened but often not. These are most familiar as the flavoring bottles behind the barista at your favorite coffeehouse. Monin, Toroni, and DaVinci are the biggest makers, although there are many smaller manufacturers as well.

6 **FROZEN FRUIT JUICE CONCENTRATES** These are the cans of frozen concentrate (orange, apple, cranberry, lemonade, limeade, and more) to which you must add water if you're making a pitcher of orange juice, apple juice, or what have you. These all must be thawed before they can be measured in a jigger. Don't chip out a frozen chunk and think you've come up with an accurate measurement. And do not substitute fruit juice or fruit syrup for concentrate. We want that powerful hit: The ice will do the diluting. By the way, some high-end supermarkets now carry *nonfrozen* fruit juice

concentrates in the beverage aisle. These will work just as well—with no thawing necessary.

7 **TRIPLE SEC** It was once the French answer to Dutch Curaçao, then it became a cheap, poorly flavored substitute for the good stuff, thanks to a range of bad '90s frozen drinks featured prominently at adult casual restaurant chains. The name doesn't mean "triple dry" but instead implies "triple distilled"—that is, it's a distilled spirit made from oranges (once a mix of bitter and sweet oranges, now much sweeter than bitter). These days, there's an astounding array on the market. Remember what your mother told you about plastic surgery and apply it here: You get what you pay for.

8 **BITTER ORANGE–FLAVORED LIQUEURS** By these, we mean higher-end orange spirits like Cointreau, usually made from bitter oranges. We call for these when we want a more nuanced, sophisticated flavor in a frozen drink than triple sec would afford. By the way, Grand Marnier is a Cognac-based orange spirit. You can indeed substitute it for any of the bitter-orange liqueurs called for in this book for a much more complex, slightly bitter flavor in the drink—not quite as refreshing, but usually more elegant. It's probably not best for deck drinks, far better for those served indoors.

9 **SWEETENED LIME JUICE** This is the bar staple: lime juice that has been rendered quite sticky with sugars, corn syrup, and/or other sweeteners. The most familiar brand is Rose's. Always refrigerate it. If it's not lime green in color, if it's even the slightest bit brown, it's oxidized; pony up for a new bottle. Or skip all that and make your own (page 41).

10 FRUIT LIQUEURS

We never call for an eau-de-vie—that is, a spirit distilled from any fruit juice other than grapes, like peach grappa or poire Williams. Instead, we call for fruit-based liqueurs: distilled spirits like brandy, vodka, or just clear alcohol, into which fruit syrups, juices, or sweeteners have been introduced. These will add both sweetness and body to a drink. The better stocked the liquor store, the wider the range you will discover.

Now that we've gone over the generalities and specifics, there's only one more thing to consider. Throughout this book, we call for some rather generic bar staples such as crème de banane (sometimes spelled crème de banana) or crème de cassis; these are flavored, sweet liqueurs made either from the real thing (bananas, black currants, etc.) or from an extract and copious amounts of sugar. However, other items like maraschino or gingerbread liqueur may be unfamiliar to you. To clarify what we intend, here's a list of specific brands. Don't feel that you have to buy the ones listed here; rather, go to a liquor store and search through the shelves. You may find one that's more to your liking.

- **bitter orange liqueur,** such as Cointreau, Patrón Citrónge, or Luxardo Triplum
- **cherry liqueur,** such as Luxardo Cherry Liqueur or Heering The Original Cherry Liqueur
- **coffee liqueur,** such as Kahlúa or Tia Maria
- **dram syrup (or pimiento dram),** such as St. Elizabeth Allspice Dram (or see page 85)
- **elderflower liqueur,** such as St-Germain
- **ginger liqueur,** such as Domaine de Canton Ginger Liqueur

- **gingerbread liqueur,** such as Art in the Age Snap

- **hazelnut liqueur,** such as Frangelico

- **maraschino liqueur,** such as Luxardo Maraschino or Lazzaroni Maraschino Liqueur

- **passion fruit liqueur,** such as Alizé Gold Passion, Bols Maracuja, or Passoã

- **peach liqueur,** such as Stirrings Peach Liqueur or peach schnapps

- **raspberry liqueur,** such as crème de framboise or Chambord

- **vanilla liqueur,** such as Licor 43, Tuaca, or Dr. McGillicuddy's Vanilla Schnapps

Armed with this knowledge, let's get to it: to blending fresher, creamier, and more innovative frozen drinks. We've divided them up into the four places we like to serve them—on the deck, in the lounge, in front of the hearth, and at a tailgate party. You can mix and match at your pleasure. Have a lounge drink on a winter night. Have a cream drink on a summer afternoon. Really, the sky's the limit, power sources permitting.

DECK

Let's start outside on the deck with frozen drinks that take full advantage of the bright sparks of flavor that only citrus, berries, and stone fruits provide. There's nothing creamy or heavy here. These drinks express the breeziness of summer.

Although few of these cocktails are classics (yet), they're based on the traditional philosophy of blender drinks before purchased mixes and corn syrup conquered the field: that a frozen drink should be more floral than sweet, that it should have a range of flavors rather than a simplified palette, and that it should be about sipping, not chugging.

Since fruit carries the day, we should mention the cardinal rule for all your fruit purchasing endeavors: If it doesn't smell like anything, chances are it won't taste like anything. Pick up those peaches, those strawberries, those blackberries and put them near (not against) your nose. Sure, everyone at the supermarket will think you're a crackpot, but you'll have the best frozen drinks on the block and they won't.

FROZEN LEMON MERINGUE PIE

Want a summery treat? With a bit of almond to mimic the crust and some brandy to reference the vanilla in the meringue, this sweet refresher tastes just like the classic dessert, no oven necessary. (Orgeat is a sweet, almond-flavored syrup laced with a little rose-flower or orange-flower water.) Don't even think about bottled lemon juice. Squeeze your own.

- 3 cups (13½ ounces) small ice cubes
- 3 ounces silver rum
- 2 ounces fresh lemon juice
- 2 ounces simple syrup, store-bought or homemade (page 25)
- 2 ounces orgeat
- 1 ounce brandy

Put all the ingredients in a large blender in the order listed. Cover and blend until smooth and rich, stopping the machine as necessary to shake down the canister, less than 1 minute. Divide between two medium glasses, preferably double old-fashioned glasses.

makes two 12-ounce drinks

GARNISH Lay a graham cracker across the top of the glass.

LIKE A PRO Sprinkle a few dashes of orange bitters on top of each drink.

FROZEN
IN THE PINK

If color is everything, here's a clarion call for attention. This sweet-tart drink has a vibrant pink color, a jewel in the glass. It's easy to slurp down but also quite sophisticated. You might want to dress for the occasion. Just don't wear white—unless you like pink polka dots.

- 3 cups (13½ ounces) small ice cubes
- 3 ounces silver tequila
- 2 ounces fresh pink grapefruit juice
- 1½ ounces grenadine, store-bought or homemade (page 37)
- 1 ounce simple syrup, store-bought or homemade (see below)
- 1 ounce elderflower liqueur
- ½ ounce fresh lime juice

Put all the ingredients in a large blender in the order listed. Cover and blend until icy and thick, stopping the machine as necessary to shake down the canister, less than 1 minute. Divide between two frozen margarita glasses.

makes two 12-ounce drinks

 Although almost all liquor stores and even supermarkets carry Simple Syrup, you can make your own. For a little over 2 cups, mix 2 cups sugar and 1 cup water in a medium saucepan. Stir over medium heat until the sugar dissolves, then bring to a simmer and cook for 1 minute. Remove the pan from the heat and cool to room temperature, about 1 hour. Pour into a glass jar or container, seal well, and store in the refrigerator for up to 4 months.

BANANAS FOSTER FREEZE

Take bananas, add caramel for a downtown twist on the classic frozen daiquiri, and you've got one of the smoothest drinks in this book. Caramel syrup is available at most liquor stores—or you can make your own for a deeper flavor with slightly bitter undertones, all the better to contrast with the banana and rum.

- 1 ripe banana, peeled and broken into pieces
- 3 cups (13½ ounces) small ice cubes
- 3 ounces silver rum
- 2 ounces crème de banane
- 1½ ounces caramel syrup (not caramel sauce), store-bought or homemade (see below)
- 1½ ounces fresh lime juice
- 1 ounce triple sec

Put all the ingredients in a large blender in the order listed. Cover and blend until smooth, about 1 minute. Pour into two 12-ounce glasses, preferably old-fashioned Coca-Cola glasses or even grandmotherly soft drink glasses.

makes two 12-ounce drinks

Here's how to make a scant 2 cups of Caramel Syrup: Bring a small saucepan of water to a boil over high heat. Meanwhile, melt 2 cups sugar in a large, high-sided saucepan, stirring with a long-handled wooden spoon only after you see evidence of melting at the edges of the pan. Continue cooking, stirring occasionally, until amber brown. Stirring all the while, add 1 cup boiling water. Be careful: The mixture will roil in the pan. Keep stirring until the sugar melts again. Remove the pan from the heat and cool to room temperature, about 2 hours. Pour into a glass container, seal well, and store in the refrigerator for up to 4 months.

LIKE A PRO
Substitute aged rum for the silver rum for a deeper caramel flavor.

SIBERIAN FRUIT SALAD

There's not much fruit in Siberia. But there is a lot of vodka. So we've linked Saint Petersburg with Novosibirsk to give you the best of both in this summery cocktail, stocked with all sorts of fruit flavors. If they'd been serving this in the gulag, Solzehnitsyn might have had more company.

- 2 cups (9 ounces) small ice cubes
- 2 ounces vodka
- 1½ ounces thawed frozen lemonade concentrate
- 1 ounce crème de banane
- 1 ounce peach liqueur (not eau-de-vie)
- 1 ounce strawberry syrup (not juice)

Put the ice cubes, vodka, lemonade concentrate, crème de banane, and peach liqueur in a large blender in that order. Cover and blend until snow cone pale white, stopping the machine as necessary to shake down the canister, less than 1 minute.

Pour ½ ounce strawberry syrup into each of two medium glasses. Divide the drink between them.

makes two 8-ounce drinks

GARNISH Use a rock candy stick as the swizzle stick.

FROZEN SUMMER PUDDING

We love summer pudding: a layered dessert of fresh berries and bread, a bombe you make a day or two in advance and turn out onto a platter. But sometimes we're lazy. We turn to the vodka and use a blender. Plus, we can skip all that bread. We could probably even make the case that this is a paleo cocktail. But as we said, we're lazy.

- 2 cups (9 ounces) small ice cubes
- ½ cup frozen raspberries
- 3 ounces vodka
- 2 ounces unsweetened pomegranate juice (not concentrate)
- 2 ounces orgeat
- ½ ounce crème de cassis
- ½ ounce sweetened lime juice, store-bought or homemade (page 41)

Put all the ingredients in a large blender in the order listed. Cover and blend until icy and thick, stopping the machine as necessary to shake down the canister, less than 1 minute. Pour into two large martini glasses.

makes two 10-ounce drinks

GARNISH
Sprinkle fresh raspberries over the drink.

STRAWBERRY RHUBARB COOLER

Since Aperol is rhubarb based, we can get a little of that flavor into this libation, a great antidote to the summer heat. The almond flavor in the amaretto gives the drink a sophisticated finish—and the salt offsets it enough that you'll want another round fairly fast.

- 1½ cups frozen hulled strawberries
- 2 ounces fresh orange juice
- 1½ ounces gin
- 1½ ounces Aperol
- 1 ounce amaretto
- ¼ teaspoon salt

Put all the ingredients in a large blender in the order listed. Cover and blend until slushy and pink, stopping the machine as necessary to shake down the canister, less than 1 minute. Divide between two large martini glasses.

makes two 7-ounce drinks

GARNISH Wet the rims of the glasses with orange juice and roll them in superfine sugar.

NIBBLE Have some Marinated Pepper Strips on hand. Slice jarred roasted red and yellow bell peppers into thin strips. Toss with minced fresh basil, aged syrupy balsamic vinegar, some finely grated orange zest, a little salt, and some pepper. Marinate at room temperature for about an hour, then fork up the strips onto toasted baguette rounds or purchased melba toast.

PEACH RASPBERRY GLACIER

Frozen peach slices stand in for the ice in this simple cooler. Best of all, they give the drink more flavor and body without any watery dilution. If the sparkling wine is chilled, it will keep both the drink thicker and preserve a little of its bubbly fizziness even after blending.

- 8 ounces frozen peach slices
- 12 ounces Prosecco, Cava, or sparkling white wine
- 2 ounces peach liqueur (not eau-de-vie)
- 1 teaspoon fresh lemon juice
- 2 ounces raspberry syrup (not juice or concentrate)

Place the peach slices, wine, peach liqueur, and lemon juice in a large blender. Cover and blend until icy and thick, less than 1 minute.

Divide the raspberry syrup between two highball glasses. Pour and spoon the frozen libation to force the syrup up the insides of the glass.

makes two 12-ounce drinks

LIKE A PRO Freeze fresh pitted peach slices (peeled or unpeeled) on a baking sheet for at least 12 hours, then transfer them to a large, sealable bag and store in the freezer for up to 3 months.

GARNISH
Slip a fresh peach slice on the rim of each glass.

NIBBLE Put out a bowl of Brown Sugar Black Pepper Almonds. Line a large baking sheet with a silicone baking mat. Warm a little vegetable oil in a large nonstick skillet set over medium heat. Add whole raw almonds and cook, stirring often, until toasted and fragrant. Add some dark brown sugar (about a tablespoon at a time), stirring until each melts, just to coat the nuts. Add a hefty bit of freshly ground black pepper and a little salt; toss well. Spread the nuts on the prepared baking sheet to cool to room temperature, about 1 hour.

MELON-BERRY-BASIL-BALSAMIC SLUSH

We've morphed the traditional flavors of a strawberry margarita into an über-summery quaff. Use individually frozen strawberries, rather than blocks of strawberries frozen in syrup. And use the good, high-quality, syrupy balsamic vinegar. Then sit back and drink in the summer light.

2 cups rindless, cubed, seedless red watermelon

2 cups frozen hulled strawberries

6 large basil leaves

3 ounces silver tequila

1 ounce triple sec

1 ounce grenadine, store-bought or homemade (page 37)

1 ounce simple syrup, store-bought or homemade (page 25)

4 teaspoons aged, syrupy balsamic vinegar

Place the watermelon, strawberries, basil, tequila, triple sec, grenadine, and simple syrup in a large blender in that order. Cover and blend until rich, red, and smooth, less than 1 minute. If the drink doesn't blend well, turn off and unplug the blender, use the handle of a wooden spoon to smash everything down, remove the spoon, cover again, and continue blending.

Pour 2 teaspoons balsamic vinegar into each of two large glasses. Pour in the slushy drink so the vinegar runs up the inside of the glasses.

makes two 14-ounce drinks

LIKE A PRO Use reposado tequila for a slightly darker, more complex flavor to match the vinegar.

SLUSHY APRICOT SOURS

Apricots lose a great deal of flavor once frozen, so we've used *both* apricot syrup and apricot brandy to craft an icy treat that's got the characteristic flavor of one of summer's best stone fruits. The texture is a little loose, so the drink is a fast guzzle unless you're careful.

- 2½ cups (11¼ ounces) small ice cubes
- 2½ ounces vodka
- 2½ ounces apricot syrup (not nectar or juice)
- 1 ounce apricot-flavored brandy
- 1 ounce fresh lemon juice

Put all the ingredients in a large blender in the order listed. Cover and blend until icy but thick, stopping the machine as necessary to shake down the canister, less than 1 minute. Divide between two large martini glasses.

makes two 9-ounce drinks

LIKE A PRO Use large thyme sprigs as swizzle sticks.

NIBBLE Have a small plate of Stuffed Peppadew Peppers on the table. Mix soft goat cheese with finely grated lemon zest and chopped, shelled pistachios. Pack into vinegary, jarred, drained peppadew peppers.

GUAI TAI

Pretty and pink, this quencher is a frozen take on a mai tai, tweaked with guava juice (instead of pineapple) and made more substantial in its flavor profile to stand up to the bulk of ice. There's no need for an expensive aged rum; you want that oaky caramelization with vanilla overtones that a sturdy but economical bottling affords.

- 3 cups (13½ ounces) small ice cubes
- 3 ounces aged rum
- 3 ounces guava nectar (not juice)
- 1½ ounces amaretto
- 1½ ounces grenadine, store-bought or homemade (see below)
- ¾ ounce triple sec
- ¾ ounce fresh lime juice
- ¾ ounce orgeat

Put all the ingredients in a large blender in the order listed. Cover and blend until smooth and thick, stopping the machine as necessary to shake down the canister, less than 1 minute. Pour into two large glasses.

makes two 12-ounce drinks

GARNISH Decorate with skewers of peeled kiwi cubes.

 Take it over the top with homemade Grenadine. Mix 2 cups unsweetened pomegranate juice and 1¾ cups sugar in a medium saucepan. Stir over medium-low heat until the sugar dissolves and the liquid is clear again. Stir in 2 tablespoons fresh lemon juice, 2 tablespoons pomegranate molasses, and 2 teaspoons rosewater. Cook, stirring constantly, until hot but do not boil. Cool and pour into a 1-quart glass container; seal and refrigerate for up to 2 months.

GARNISH
Stick gummy grapefruit candy slices on the glasses.

FROZEN GRAPEFRUIT WHISKEY SOURS

Cooling and sophisticated, this frozen treat morphs the classic cocktail into an icy slush. Don't use standard grapefruit juice—it won't have enough oomph to stand up to the other ingredients. The grapefruit shrub adds a slight vinegar taste, adult and satisfying. You'll find bottled shrubs at well-stocked liquor stores or through online suppliers.

2½ cups (11¼ ounces) small ice cubes

3 ounces rye or Canadian whisky

1½ ounces grapefruit shrub, store-bought or homemade (page 40)

1 ounce thawed frozen grapefruit concentrate

1 ounce triple sec

½ ounce fresh lime juice

½ ounce simple syrup, store-bought or homemade (page 25)

Put all the ingredients in a large blender in the order listed. Cover and blend until thick and icy off-white, stopping the machine as necessary to shake down the canister, less than 1 minute. Divide between two double old-fashioned glasses.

makes two 10-ounce drinks

CONTINUES

DIY EXCESS To make your own Grapefruit Shrub, use a vegetable peeler to remove the zest and even some of the rind from a large ruby-red grapefruit. Cut the fruit into supremes (see page 63), then place the zest and rind, the supremes, and any caught juice in a large glass jar. Add 1 cup sugar and muddle well. Seal and store at room temperature overnight (for at least 10 hours but not more than 16 hours). Add 1 cup distilled white vinegar, stir well, cover, and refrigerate for 1 week, shaking the jar daily. After a week, strain into a large bowl, pressing on the solids to extract every drop of juice. You'll end up with a scant 2 cups grapefruit shrub. Pour the juice into a clean glass jar, seal, and store in the refrigerator for up to 6 months.

MANGO SNAP

We were sitting out on the deck one summer afternoon, eating a scoop of mango sorbet with a gingersnap cookie on the side, when it hit us. "This should be a drink," we said. Inspiration comes from many sources. Including dessert.

- 1½ cups (6¾ ounces) small ice cubes
- ½ cup mango sorbet
- 1 ounce vodka
- 1 ounce ginger liqueur
- 1 ounce cinnamon schnapps
- ½ ounce sweetened lime juice, store-bought or homemade (see below)

Put all the ingredients in a large blender in the order listed. Cover and blend until slushy and thick, less than 1 minute. Divide between martini glasses.

makes two 6-ounce drinks

LIKE A PRO Substitute 2 ounces Art of the Age Snap gingersnap liqueur for the ginger liqueur and the cinnamon schnapps.

DIY EXCESS Make your own Sweetened Lime Juice. Mix ¾ cup sugar and ½ cup water in a medium saucepan set over medium heat, stirring until the liquid is clear. Continue cooking without stirring until small bubbles fizz at the inside rim of the pan, 1 to 2 minutes. Remove from the heat and cool to room temperature, about 2 hours. Stir in 1½ cups lime juice, then pour into a 1-quart glass jar or plastic container, cover, and refrigerate for up to 1 month.

GARNISH Use a cinnamon stick as a swizzle stick.

FROZEN ZOMBIES

Despite what Hollywood thinks, Zombies are a fruit-laced and Falernum drink, heavy on the rum. Very heavy—they were once also known as Skull Punchers. Don the Beachcomber, one of the classic tiki restaurants of the '70s, limited its customers to two Zombies per evening. We've lightened the liquor a bit and frozen the whole concoction, so feel free to have more if the sun is blazing outside.

- 3 cups (13½ ounces) small ice cubes
- 3 ounces aged rum
- 1 ounce fresh lemon juice
- 1 ounce fresh lime juice
- 1 ounce simple syrup, store-bought or homemade (page 25)
- ½ ounce apricot-flavored brandy
- ½ ounce Falernum, store-bought or homemade (page 69)
- ½ ounce grenadine, store-bought or homemade (page 37)
- Pinch of ground cinnamon

Put all the ingredients in a large blender in the order listed. Cover and blend until pale pink and smooth, stopping the machine as necessary to shake down the canister, less than 1 minute. Divide between two large glasses.

makes two 12-ounce drinks

FROZEN GODZILLAS

Midori is a muskmelon-flavored Japanese liqueur (*midori* in Japanese means "green"). Here, we've spiked it with the tart zing of lemonade, then mellowed the whole thing with orange notes. If you have two of these cocktails, you may actually go on a rampage and pull the roof off your house. Don't say you weren't warned.

- 3 cups (13½ ounces) small ice cubes
- 1½ ounces vodka
- 1½ ounces Midori
- 1½ ounces thawed frozen lemonade concentrate
- ¾ ounce triple sec
- ¾ ounce thawed orange juice concentrate
- ¾ ounce simple syrup, store-bought or homemade (page 25)

Place all the ingredients in a large blender in the order listed. Cover and blend until a pale-green slush, stopping the machine as necessary to shake down the canister, less than 1 minute. Divide between two large glasses.

makes two 12-ounce drinks

NIBBLE Bake up some Bacon Skewers. Thread thin strips of bacon onto bamboo skewers, piercing each several times. Brush with maple syrup and sprinkle with cracked black peppercorns. Bake on a large rimmed baking sheet in a 375°F oven for 15 minutes or until browned.

GEORGIA
ICE STORM

The peach tree state needs a state cocktail: May we suggest this? The slight amount of vinegar in the shrub turns the drink ridiculously refreshing, the antidote to a Down South heat wave. Look for peach shrubs at well-stocked liquor stores or through online suppliers.

- 2½ cups (11¼ ounces) small ice cubes
- 2 ounces silver rum
- 2 ounces peach shrub, store-bought or homemade (see below)
- 1 ounce aged rum
- 1 ounce peach liqueur (not eau-de-vie)
- 1 ounce simple syrup, store-bought or homemade (page 25)
- ¼ teaspoon vanilla extract

Put all the ingredients in a large blender in the order listed. Cover and blend until slushy and thick, stopping the machine as necessary to shake down the canister, less than 1 minute. Divide between two double old-fashioned glasses.

makes two 11-ounce drinks

DIY EXCESS To make your own Peach Shrub, pit and chop 1 pound peaches. Put these in a large glass container and mix with 1 cup sugar until coated. Cover and refrigerate for 2 days, stirring occasionally until the sugar has dissolved and the peaches have given off liquid. Add 1 cup white wine vinegar, stir well, cover, and refrigerate for 1 week. Strain through a fine-mesh sieve lined with cheesecloth into a large bowl. Discard the solids. Pour into a 1-quart glass jar, seal, and refrigerate for up to 2 months.

LOUNGE

Put on your skinny tie and come inside for cool drinks with a downtown vibe. Some are retro cocktails morphed into frozen potations. Most have a less sweet finish, more befitting evening than afternoon. All offer a wider array of flavor notes than our deck cocktails; you'll even find bitter and herbaceous accents.

If you've got a lounge party going, don't be lashed to the blender. Prep the ingredients in advance, mixing the juices and liquors together in small bowls, one bowl per recipe. Just add the ice to the blender and dump in a single batch of the necessary mixture.

Because there are more nuanced flavors here, you'll need to make sure you bring your A game to the bar. Not all the ice and juice in the world can cover the taste of cheap vodka, gin, or rum. While you don't have to work with an aged, sipping spirit or microdistiller hooch, you do want to use a bottling you'd drink on its own.

Then sit back and relish the lounge life. Put on some Dean Martin or Frank Sinatra. With a frozen drink in hand, life's chill.

ICY SIDECAR

We love retro cocktails. But let's face it: A sidecar can be a sledgehammer, a hard hit of alcohol and lemon juice. We've softened the whole thing for the blender, turning it into a luscious concoction with just a slight pucker. Finally, a sidecar you can quaff!

- 2½ cups (11¼ ounces) small ice cubes
- 2½ ounces thawed frozen lemonade concentrate
- 1½ ounces brandy
- 1½ ounces bourbon
- 1 ounce bitter orange liqueur

Put all the ingredients in a large blender in the order listed. Cover and blend until a pale, off-white, semifrozen snow cone, stopping the machine as necessary to shake the blender canister, less than 1 minute. Pour into two martini glasses.

makes two 10-ounce drinks

GARNISH Coat the rims of the glasses in decorative sanding sugar before pouring the drink. Go all out with festive colors.

NIBBLE Make a Salty Snack Mix. Melt a little unsalted butter in the microwave, then pour it into a large bowl and mix in pretzel nuggets and oyster crackers, as well as a splash of Worcestershire sauce, a little Old Bay seasoning, and several dashes of hot red pepper sauce. Toss well, then spread onto a rimmed baking sheet and bake in a 250°F oven for about 45 minutes, stirring every 15 minutes.

FROZEN JUNE BUG

You can't just take a classic cocktail, add ice, and turn it into a frozen drink. You'll water it down. You have to account for all that slush. In this case, we use pineapple-flavored ice cubes to keep the drink cold and strong. Make more pineapple cubes than you need and keep them around all season. Use 1½ cups (or 6¾ ounces) of pineapple ice cubes (as well as the same amount of small ice cubes) each time you make this recipe.

⅔ cup unsweetened pineapple juice
1½ cups (6¾ ounces) small ice cubes
3 ounces vodka
2 ounces Midori
1 ounce Galliano
1 ounce sweetened cream of coconut (not coconut milk)
1 ounce liquid from a jar of maraschino cherries (page 97)

Pour the pineapple juice into ice cube trays and freeze until hard, for at least 24 hours or up to 2 months.

Mix the pineapple juice ice cubes with the regular ice cubes in a large blender, add the vodka, Midori, Galliano, and cream of coconut. Cover and blend until slushy but thick, stopping the machine as necessary to shake down the canister, less than 1 minute.

Pour ½ ounce maraschino cherry juice into each of two tall glasses. Divide the frozen drink between the glasses.

makes two 12-ounce drinks

GARNISH Float a maraschino cherry on top of each drink.

SLOE FREEZER BURN

Sweet and tart take a road trip south of the border in this tequila-based mash-up, part margarita, part retro cocktail, doused with sloe gin (and thus flavored with sloe plums). It's definitely a hot-weather quencher for indoors, with tropical notes and a surprisingly complex balance of flavors.

2½ cups (11¼ ounces) small ice cubes
2 ounces silver tequila
1 ounce sloe gin
1 ounce thawed frozen cranberry juice concentrate
1 ounce fresh lime juice
1 ounce caramel syrup (not caramel sauce), store-bought or homemade (page 26)
½ ounce crème de banane

Put all the ingredients in a large blender in the order listed. Cover and blend until a slushy, red wonder, stopping the machine as necessary to shake down the canister, less than 1 minute. Divide between two large glasses, perhaps classic Coca-Cola glasses. Or keep the blender canister on ice and serve in shots for your favorite drinking game.

makes two 10-ounce drinks

SPANISH FROST

Amontillado is a yeasty version of sherry, aged until it's a mellow brown color—an out-of-favor drink favored by great aunts. So it's a bit of a surprise in a nouveau frozen libation. It pairs well with sweeter bourbon to make this hip but fairly simple frozen cocktail. Your elders won't know what's come over you (but they'll like it).

- 2½ cups (11¼ ounces) small ice cubes
- 2½ ounces Amontillado sherry
- 2 ounces bourbon
- 1½ ounces simple syrup, store-bought or homemade (page 25)
- 1½ ounces fresh lemon juice

Put all the ingredients in a large blender in the order listed. Cover and blend until smooth and pale brown, stopping the machine as necessary to shake down the canister, less than 1 minute. Divide between two large glasses.

makes two 8-ounce drinks

CHILLY LEMON DROP

Can the '90s be retro? (Have you been to Silicon Valley?) Back then, the lemon drop was all the rage in cocktail lounges frequented by dot-com geeks. These days, we're not much for wool vests over white T-shirts and we like our drinks slushy rather than lukewarm. So we've revamped the once-chic with bigger flavors and more chill for a modern, hipster-geek vibe. Don't get any caught in your beard.

- 2 cups (9 ounces) small ice cubes
- 3 ounces vodka
- 1½ ounces simple syrup, store-bought or homemade (page 25)
- 1½ ounces fresh lemon juice
- 1 ounce limoncello

Put all the ingredients in a large blender in the order listed. Cover and blend until smooth and thick, stopping the machine as necessary to shake down the canister, less than 1 minute. Pour into large martini glasses.

makes two 8-ounce drinks

LIKE A PRO Use fresh Meyer lemon juice, rather than standard lemon juice.

NIBBLE Have some Rosemary Hummus on the side. Mix drained and rinsed canned chickpeas with some tahini and lemon juice, as well as a little fresh rosemary and minced garlic, a generous pour of olive oil, and some salt and pepper in a large food processor. Cover and process until smooth, adding more olive oil as necessary to create a creamy consistency. Scrape into a bowl and serve with flatbread crackers.

FROZEN APEROL SPRITZ

Toast just about anything with this refreshing, sophisticated slushy. You'll stir in some additional Prosecco after making the drink, so there's a slight touch of post-blend fizz for the bubble lovers. Have more of the ingredients right nearby. You'll want another round.

- 1 cup lemon sorbet
- 6 ounces (¾ cup) chilled Prosecco, Cava, or sparkling wine
- 1 ounce Aperol

Place the sorbet and 4 ounces (½ cup) Prosecco in a large blender. Cover and blend until smooth, less than 1 minute. Uncover and add the remainder of the Prosecco, stirring gently with the handle of a wooden spoon to preserve the bubbles.

Pour ½ ounce Aperol into each of two champagne flutes. Divide the frozen drink between the flutes.

makes two 8-ounce drinks

FROST ON THE GIN BLOSSOM

You'll need super-tart passion fruit concentrate (not passion fruit juice, nectar, or syrup) to make this bright, sweet-tart, icy libation. Passion fruit concentrate is available in jars in the freezer section of high-end supermarkets or from many outlets online.

- 3 cups (13½ ounces) small ice cubes
- 3 ounces gin
- 2 ounces fresh orange juice
- 1½ ounces simple syrup, store-bought or homemade (page 25)
- 1 ounce bitter orange liqueur
- 1 ounce thawed frozen passion fruit concentrate (not juice)
- ½ ounce fresh lime juice

Put all the ingredients in a large blender in the order listed. Cover and blend until smooth, stopping the machine as necessary to shake down the canister, less than 1 minute. Divide between two large glasses.

makes two 12-ounce drinks

GARNISH Plant an edible flower like a nasturtium in each drink.

> **NIBBLE** For Savory Warm Olives, mix brine-cured green olives, olive oil, finely grated orange zest, a sprinkling of fennel seeds, and a cinnamon stick in a small baking dish. Warm in a 350°F oven until fragrant, 15 to 20 minutes, stirring occasionally. Serve warm or at room temperature.

ICY APPLE TWANG

Spicy and refreshing, this frozen libation has hints of ginger, orange, and even vinegar (from the shrub), reminiscent of a good apple pie. In fact, think of this as our take on apple pie filling. Except with vodka. You're welcome.

- 2 cups (9 ounces) small ice cubes
- 2 ounces thawed frozen apple juice concentrate
- 2 ounces vodka
- 1 ounce triple sec
- ½ ounce ginger shrub, store-bought or homemade (see below)

Put all the ingredients in a large blender in the order listed. Cover and blend until slushy, smooth, and pale white, stopping the machine as necessary to shake down the canister, less than 1 minute. Pour into two medium glasses.

makes two 8-ounce drinks

 Make Ginger Shrub yourself. Combine 1 cup apple cider vinegar and ½ cup chopped, peeled fresh ginger in a small saucepan set over medium-high heat. Cook just until bubbles fizz around the inner edge of the pan. Pour into a glass jar, cover, and set aside at room temperature for 24 hours. Strain through cheesecloth without pressing or squeezing, catching the liquid in a bowl below. Add enough white wine vinegar to the liquid to equal ⅔ cup total. Pour into a small saucepan, stir in ⅔ cup sugar, and heat, stirring occasionally, until the sugar dissolves. Continue cooking only until the liquid turns clear. Remove from the heat and cool to room temperature. Pour back into that cleaned glass jar, cover, and refrigerate for up to 2 months.

BLUEBERRY NUMB-BELLINI

Depending on how fast you down it, you might need iced-tea spoons to get every last drop of this thick, rich concoction, a fusion of berries and sparkling wine. Then again, you might not be able to operate the spoons properly with the ensuing brain freeze.

- 1½ cups (6¾ ounces) small ice cubes
- 6 ounces (¾ cup) sparkling white wine
- ½ cup frozen blueberries
- ½ ounce crème de cassis
- ½ ounce simple syrup, store-bought or homemade (page 25)
- 1 teaspoon fresh lime juice

Put all the ingredients in a large blender in the order listed. Cover and blend until smooth and dark purple, stopping the machine as necessary to shake down the canister, less than 1 minute. Divide between two champagne flutes.

makes two 8-ounce drinks

CAMPARI GRAPEFRUIT CHILL

This frozen drink has a slightly bitter taste from the grapefruit, gin, Campari, *and* black currant liqueur (or crème de cassis). Sure, there's enough simple syrup to take off the edge, but the results have a sophisticated feel (even when frozen). Look for packed, fresh grapefruit supremes in the refrigerator case of your supermarket's produce section. Avoid the canned supremes that have way less punch.

3 cups (13½ ounces) small ice cubes
1 cup juice-packed pink grapefruit supremes
2½ ounces gin
2 ounces Campari
2 ounces simple syrup, store-bought or homemade (page 25)
½ ounce crème de cassis

Place the ice cubes, grapefruit, gin, Campari, and simple syrup in a large blender in that order. Cover and blend until smooth and pale pink, stopping the machine as necessary to shake down the canister, less than 1 minute.

Divide the crème de cassis between two large glasses. Pour the drink into the glasses, letting the crème de cassis crawl up the insides of the glass.

makes two 14-ounce drinks

GARNISH Hang a cluster of seedless black grapes—or better yet, black currants—on each glass.

DIY EXCESS Here's how to make your own Grapefruit Supremes. Cut a small slice off a grapefruit's top and bottom so the round fruit can stand steadily on the counter. Use a sharp paring knife to cut the rind off the flesh in long arcs, starting at the top and following down the natural curve of the fruit. Cut far enough into the flesh to remove the white pith but not so far as to damage the pulp. Once peeled, hold the fruit in one hand over your serving bowl, then use that paring knife to cut between the flesh and the white membranes separating the individual segments, allowing these to fall into the bowl along with any juice. Discard any membranes, the pith, and the rind so you're left with the bright pink, jewel-like, half-moon bits of grapefruit bliss. One large pink grapefruit will make about 1 cup supremes and juice.

NIBBLE Have a plate of Bacon-Wrapped Figs on the side. Stem fresh Black Mission or green Calimyrna figs, then halve them through the stem ends. Wrap each fig half in one thin strip of bacon. Set on a large rimmed baking sheet and bake in a 375°F oven until the bacon is crisp and the figs are soft, 12 to 15 minutes. Cool a few minutes before serving.

FUZZY BLACK CURRANT FREEZE

You'll be surprised how chic a frozen drink can be when you add a bitter undertone amidst the sweet notes—that is, the black currant flavor to the peach and orange palette. Keep the ice cubes in the freezer until you're ready to blend them to keep the drink from separating too quickly.

- 2½ cups (11¼ ounces) small ice cubes
- 2½ ounces gin
- 2 ounces black currant or cassis syrup (not black currant juice or liqueur)
- 1 ounce fresh lemon juice
- ¾ ounce peach liqueur (not eau-de-vie)
- ¾ ounce triple sec

Put all the ingredients in a large blender in the order listed. Cover and blend until thick and delicious, stopping the machine as necessary to shake down the canister, less than 1 minute. Divide between two highball glasses.

makes two 9-ounce drinks

GARNISH Put multicolored citrus wheels on the rim of the glass: lemon, orange, and lime.

NIBBLE Make Warm Chinese Cashews. Warm unsalted cashews with a little toasted sesame oil in a large skillet set over medium-low heat, stirring often, until very fragrant. Add a sprinkling of five-spice powder and a small splash of soy sauce. Cook, stirring all the time, until the pan is dry. Serve warm.

ANDEAN GLACIER

Pisco is a distilled grape brandy from Chile or Peru. (Don't start trying to figure out which country invented the stuff unless you're hankering for a war.) The traditional Pisco Sour is made with an egg white—which gives this frozen version an unbelievable creaminess. Since you're working with raw eggs, use pasteurized eggs or eggs from a local farmer you trust.

1 cup (4½ ounces) small ice cubes
1 large egg white
3 ounces pisco
2 ounces simple syrup, store-bought or homemade (page 25)
1½ ounces fresh lemon juice
8 dashes bitters, preferably Angostura or Peychaud bitters

Place the ice cubes, egg white, pisco, simple syrup, and lemon juice in a large blender in that order. Cover and blend until frothy and light, stopping the machine as necessary to shake down the canister, less than 1 minute.

Divide the drink between two martini glasses. Dot the top of each with four drops of bitters.

makes two 8-ounce drinks

FIG AND FALERNUM FROZEN DAIQUIRI

Talk about chic sophistication! This cocktail takes the classic frozen daiquiri and pushes it to new heights with both Falernum (a retro, almond-and-spices syrup still favored in rum drinks in Barbados) and fig bitters. Both are specialty products you can find at high-end supermarkets, well-stocked liquor stores, or from suppliers online.

- 2 cups (9 ounces) small ice cubes
- 2 ounces aged rum
- 1 ounce silver rum
- 1 ounce fresh lime juice
- 1 ounce simple syrup, store-bought or homemade (page 25)
- ½ ounce Falernum, store-bought or homemade (page 69)
- 8 drops fig bitters

Put all the ingredients in a large blender in the order listed. Cover and blend until smooth and slushy, stopping the machine as necessary to shake down the canister, less than 1 minute. Divide between two white wine glasses (preferably stemless).

makes two 8-ounce drinks

GARNISH
Set half a fresh fig on the rim of each glass.

Here's how to make Falernum. Toast ½ cup sliced or slivered almonds in a large skillet over medium-low heat until browned and fragrant, 3 to 4 minutes, stirring occasionally. Cool for 20 minutes, then place in a 1-quart jar. Crush a whole nutmeg under a heavy saucepan and put about a quarter to a half of it plus 6 allspice berries in a mortar with a pestle; grind until chunky then add to the jar. Also add 30 whole cloves, ⅓ cup grated fresh ginger (no need to peel), the zest of 4 limes, and the zest of 3 lemons. Pour in ¾ cup ovenproof rum, such as Wray & Nephew White or Bacardi 151. Stir gently, cover, and set aside for 48 hours. Line a fine-mesh sieve with cheesecloth or a large coffee filter, pour the contents of the jar into the prepared sieve, and set aside to drip slowly for about 4 hours. Gently squeeze the pulpy ingredients still in the cheesecloth or filter over the sieve to remove the last drops, then pour the distilled Falernum into a clean jar. Mix 1 cup water and 1 cup sugar in a small saucepan set over medium-low heat and stir until the sugar dissolves. Heat just until bubbles begin to form at the rim of the pan. Pour into the Falernum distillate and cool to room temperature. Seal and refrigerate for up to 2 months.

POMEGRANATE FREEZE

It's like the deck moved indoors with this cooler. For the best flavor, skip the pomegranate juice and use its concentrate, often available near the fruit juices in grocery stores and, if not, in health food stores and through online retailers. It'll give enough body to punch up this refresher, a chic libation with brandy and bitter orange liqueur.

- 3 cups (13½ ounces) small ice cubes
- 3 ounces silver tequila
- 2 ounces simple syrup, store-bought or homemade (page 25)
- 1½ ounces pomegranate juice concentrate (if frozen, then thawed)
- 1½ ounces brandy
- ¾ ounce bitter orange liqueur
- ¾ ounce sweetened lime juice, store-bought or homemade (page 41)

Put all the ingredients in a large blender in the order listed. Cover and blend until smooth if still icy, stopping the machine as necessary to shake down the canister, less than 1 minute. Pour into two highball glasses.

makes two 10-ounce drinks

GARNISH Sprinkle pomegranate seeds over the drinks.

FROZEN GREEN WITH ENVY

Don't get green. Get even—by living well with a great, vibrant green drink in hand. This one's intense and fruity, a fine, refreshing mix to mellow out an evening at home. Make sure you crow on Facebook to instill the proper envy in others.

- 2 cups (9 ounces) small ice cubes
- 2 medium kiwifruit, peeled and quartered
- 3 ounces silver rum
- 1 ounce fresh lime juice
- 1 ounce simple syrup, store-bought or homemade (page 25)
- ½ ounce vanilla liqueur
- ½ ounce Midori

Put all the ingredients in a large blender in the order listed. Cover and blend until smooth, green, and speckled, stopping the machine as necessary to shake the canister, less than 1 minute. Divide between two hurricane glasses.

makes two 11-ounce drinks

GARNISH
Skewer honeydew melon balls for a swizzle stick.

LIKE A PRO Remove the white core from the kiwi fruit before blending.

PASSION-FLOWER POWER

If there ever was a drink that crossed the threshold between deck and lounge, here it is: a sweet-tart mix of fruity flavors with a splash of elderflower liqueur to give it a more elegant vibe.

- 2 cups (9 ounces) small ice cubes
- 2 ounces vodka
- 2 ounces passion fruit liqueur
- 1½ ounces thawed frozen cranberry juice concentrate
- 1 ounce elderflower liqueur
- 1 ounce simple syrup, store-bought or homemade (page 25)
- ½ ounce fresh lime juice

Put all the ingredients in a large blender in the order listed. Cover and blend until a vibrant pink slush, stopping the machine as necessary to shake down the canister, less than 1 minute. Divide between two tall glasses.

makes two 9-ounce drinks

LIKE A PRO Coordinate the drink to your wardrobe. Use Alizé Red Passion for a vibrant red drink or Alizé Blue Passion for a lavender slush.

HEARTH

These are the creamy drinks made with ice cream, sherbet, or sorbet. Yes, and cream too. We haven't forgotten it. But in truth, we haven't used it all that much. Cream has a certain mouth-shellacking quality that doesn't always translate into a good cocktail, all the White Russians in the world notwithstanding. Instead, we've let gelato and a host of other creamy frozen concoctions do the heavy lifting.

Work with high-quality ice cream, sorbet, or what have you. Lower-end frozen treats are stocked with whipped-in air. They're not very dense; they often melt into a foamy mess. They'll do that in your drink too. Enough said.

All these cocktails are best sipped, not guzzled. Unless you haven't had dinner. In which case, you'll be able to put that cliché about life being short and eating dessert first to good use.

In any event, stoke the fire and settle in. Or take a drink out to the deck for Christmas in July. Put on a holiday album. The neighbors won't mind.

VERMONT BLIZZARD

We've learned this the hard way: You have to love winter to live in New England. Even when it's summer, you have to keep doing things that remind you of winter. Like washing storm windows. Otherwise, December will come as such a big surprise you'll end up in a straitjacket. Making this maple-laced, creamy, thick shake is a much better wintervention than snowshoeing on the grass.

> 3 cups (13½ ounces) small ice cubes
> 3 ounces vodka
> 2 ounces maple syrup
> 2 ounces light cream
> 1 ounce vanilla liqueur
> ⅛ teaspoon salt

Put all the ingredients in a large blender in the order listed. Cover and blend until creamy and thick, stopping the machine as necessary to shake down the canister, less than 1 minute. Divide between two tall glasses.

makes two 14-ounce drinks

LIKE A PRO Use Grade B maple syrup, a stronger taste with more herbal notes. (And if you dare use maple-flavored pancake syrup, an entire region of the country will take up arms against you.)

BOURBON SUGAR SHAKE

Don't swipe the best bourbon in the house for this frozen nightcap (or daycap—we won't judge). Instead, splurge on the best ice cream: a small, artisanal pint. Stoke the fire. You're gonna need a minute.

- 1 cup vanilla gelato or premium ice cream
- 2 cups (9 ounces) small ice cubes
- 2 ounces bourbon
- 2 ounces coffee liqueur
- 1 ounce caramel syrup (not caramel sauce), store-bought or homemade (page 26)

Put all the ingredients in a large blender in the order listed. Cover and blend until smooth and creamy white, stopping the machine as necessary to shake down the canister, less than 1 minute. Pour into two short, squat glasses.

makes two 10-ounce drinks

 To make the best-ever Vanilla Gelato, beat 7 large egg yolks, ½ cup plus 2 tablespoons sugar, 2 tablespoons vanilla extract, and ¼ teaspoon salt in a medium bowl with an electric mixer at medium speed until thick and pale yellow, about 3 minutes. Heat 2¾ cups whole milk and ¼ cup heavy cream in a medium saucepan over medium heat until warm (do not boil), then beat about one-third of the hot milk mixture into the egg yolk mixture until smooth. Beat this combined mixture into the remaining milk mixture in the pan, then warm over very low heat, stirring constantly, until thickened, 7 to 10 minutes or until a clean instant-read meat thermometer inserted into the mixture without touching the pan registers 168°F. Strain into a bowl and refrigerate for at least 4 hours or up to 2 days. Freeze in an ice-cream maker according to the manufacturer's instructions.

MEXICAN MUDSLIDE

There's probably a TGI Fridays somewhere on the Mexican Riviera. Or there should be, if only so they can serve this drink. It's lusciously thick with layers of flavor from chocolate, coffee, cream, caramel, and coconut—the five dessert food groups.

- 2 cups (9 ounces) small ice cubes
- ¾ cup chocolate gelato or premium chocolate ice cream
- 2 ounces coconut rum
- 2 ounces coffee liqueur
- 1 ounce silver rum
- 1 ounce chocolate syrup (not hot fudge sauce), store-bought or homemade (page 81)
- ¼ teaspoon ground cinnamon
- 2 ounces caramel ice cream sauce

Place the ice cubes, ice cream, coconut rum, coffee liqueur, silver rum, chocolate syrup, and ground cinnamon in a large blender in that order. Cover and blend until like a thick shake, stopping the machine as necessary to shake down the canister, less than 1 minute.

Divide the caramel sauce between two large glasses, swirling it to coat the insides (if unevenly). Pour and spoon the drink into the two glasses.

GARNISH
Sprinkle the top of each drink with salted peanuts.

makes two 12-ounce drinks

DIY EXCESS

Here's how to make your own Chocolate Syrup. Whisk ¾ cup unsweetened cocoa powder, ¾ cup sugar, ¾ cup water, and ¼ teaspoon salt in a large saucepan set over medium-high heat until smooth. Bring to a boil, whisking often. Reduce the heat to medium-low and simmer for 2½ minutes exactly, whisking regularly. The sauce will be thin. Remove from the heat and stir in 2 teaspoons vanilla extract. The sauce will thicken as it cools. Cool to room temperature, then scrape into a glass jar or plastic container, cover, and refrigerate for up to 2 weeks.

FROZEN NUTS

Who doesn't love warm nuts? They're the epitome of first-class airline travel. (Also, you've got a dirty mind.) So where does a tall glass of frozen nuts put us? In a really good mood. Listen, if they serve this mix of ice cream, brandy, and hazelnuts in coach, we'll gladly sit in the back of the plane.

- 2 cups (9 ounces) small ice cubes
- ¾ cup butter pecan ice cream
- 1 ounce brandy
- 1 ounce aged rum
- 1 ounce hazelnut liqueur
- 1 ounce vanilla liqueur
- 1 ounce vanilla syrup (not vanilla extract)

Put all the ingredients in a large blender in the order listed. Cover and blend until creamy off-white with flecks of pecans, stopping the machine as necessary to shake down the canister, less than 1 minute. Pour into two large glasses.

makes two 11-ounce drinks

GARNISH
Serve with pecan sandy cookies.

NUT NOG

How many times have you wished that eggnog was a frozen blender drink with nuts in the mix? Okay, never. But it turns out, it's really good. If you don't think so after tasting this cocktail, write our publisher and complain. They'd love to hear from you.

- 2 cups (9 ounces) small ice cubes
- 2 ounces bourbon
- 1 ounce hazelnut liqueur
- 1 ounce simple syrup, store-bought or homemade (page 25)
- 1 ounce light cream
- ½ ounce dram syrup (or pimiento dram), store-bought or homemade (page 85)

Put all the ingredients in a large blender in the order listed. Cover and blend until thick and irresistible, stopping the machine as necessary to shake down the canister, less than 1 minute. Pour into two red wine glasses.

makes two 11-ounce drinks

LIKE A PRO Use 1 ounce bourbon and 1 ounce brandy.

GARNISH
Use long cinnamon sticks as swizzle sticks.

NIBBLE Make a hit with White Chocolate Potato Chips. Melt chopped white chocolate in a double boiler set over about an inch of slowly simmering water, stirring until smooth. Remove the top half of the double boiler from the hot water and stir in a pinch of ground cinnamon and grated nutmeg. Dip thick-cut, fluted potato chips until half submerged in the melted white chocolate, shake off any excess, and place on a large sheet of wax paper. While warm, sprinkle with chopped pistachios. Cool to room temperature.

VERY ICED COFFEE

Skip the chain-based, surly-barista-ed coffeehouse and head home to make your own decadent frozen shake, chock-full of real ice cream and dark espresso. And vodka. And bourbon. And coffee liqueur. Those are the things that a barista will never give you.

- 2 cups (9 ounces) small ice cubes
- ¾ cup premium vanilla ice cream or gelato
- 2 ounces vodka
- 1½ ounces cooled espresso
- 1 ounce coffee liqueur
- 1 ounce bourbon
- 1 ounce simple syrup, store-bought or homemade (page 25)

Put all the ingredients in a large blender in the order listed. Cover and blend until rich and smooth, stopping the machine as necessary to shake down the canister, less than 1 minute. Divide between two large brandy snifters and serve with spoons.

makes two 10-ounce drinks

GARNISH Dollop a little sweetened whipped cream on each drink.

> NIBBLE You can't go wrong with Brownie S'mores. Cut purchased or homemade brownies into the shape of graham crackers. Cover the top of the brownies with mini marshmallows and broil on a large baking sheet 4 to 6 inches from the broiler element just until the marshmallows begin to melt, less than 1 minute. Remove from the oven and press graham crackers onto the marshmallows, sealing them to the brownies.

DRAMSICLE

What do pot roast, ketchup, and this frozen shake have in common? Believe it or not, allspice. The orange-vanilla combo here is complemented with dram syrup, an old-fashioned allspice concoction that was once a staple in rum-based cocktails. It adds a woody, herbal note, a bit of depth in the sweet drink. You can buy dram syrup (also called pimiento dram) from suppliers online or well-stocked liquor stores—or you can make your own.

- ½ cup (2¼ ounces) small ice cubes
- ⅓ cup premium vanilla ice cream or gelato
- ⅓ cup orange sherbet
- 2 ounces aged rum
- 1 ounce caramel syrup (not caramel sauce), store-bought or homemade (page 26)
- ½ ounce dram syrup, store-bought or homemade (see below)

Put all the ingredients in a large blender in the order listed. Cover and blend until smooth and thick, stopping the machine as necessary to shake down the canister, less than 1 minute. Divide between two large glasses.

makes two 7-ounce drinks

GARNISH

Place an orange slice or wedge on the rim of each glass.

DIY EXCESS Make your own Dram Syrup. Mix ¼ cup crushed allspice berries with 1 cup overproof bourbon, such as Booker's, in a glass jar. Cover and set aside at room temperature for 4 days. Mix 1 cup packed dark brown sugar and 1 cup water in a small saucepan set over medium heat, stirring until the brown sugar dissolves. Continue cooking just until bubbles fizz inside the rim of the pan. Set aside to cool to room temperature, about 2 hours. Strain the liquid in the jar through a fine-mesh sieve lined with cheesecloth or a large coffee filter. Squeeze gently to get the last drops from the allspice berries. Mix with the brown sugar simple syrup and store in a covered glass jar in the fridge for up to 2 months.

BLACK FOREST FREEZE

Maybe you missed that semester abroad at the University of Freiburg in Breisgau, so we're here to fill you in. Germans love chocolate and cherries together. We made it better with vodka and brandy. Class dismissed.

- 2 cups (9 ounces) small ice cubes
- ⅔ cup premium chocolate ice cream or gelato
- 2 ounces vodka
- 2 ounces brandy
- 2 ounces sweet cherry syrup (not sour cherry syrup)

Put all the ingredients in a large blender in the order listed. Cover and blend until smooth, stopping the machine as necessary to shake down the canister, less than 1 minute. Divide between two large glasses.

makes two 8-ounce drinks

GARNISH Float a maraschino cherry in the glass.

COCONUT TORTONI

Tortoni is a classic Italian frozen dessert, a rich ice cream topped with toasted coconut and a cherry. We've morphed that into a frozen drink, the cherry liqueur painting the creamy white drink a pale pink.

- 2 cups (9 ounces) small ice cubes
- ¾ cup coconut sorbet
- 2 ounces vodka
- 1½ ounces caramel syrup (not caramel sauce), store-bought or homemade (page 26)
- 1 ounce silver rum
- ½ teaspoon vanilla extract
- 1 ounce cherry liqueur

Place the ice cubes, sorbet, vodka, syrup, rum, and vanilla extract in a large blender in that order. Cover and blend until slushy but smooth, stopping the machine as necessary to shake down the canister, less than 1 minute.

Place ½ ounce cherry liqueur in each of two double old-fashioned glasses. Divide the drink between the glasses.

makes two 10-ounce drinks

GARNISH Once again, maraschino cherries in the glass. Extra points if you can tie the stem into a knot with your tongue.

SALT CARAMEL SLUSH

Whoever first put salt and caramel together ought to win the Nobel Prize for Food. Whoever thought of mixing that combo with vodka and brandy in a frozen drink ought to get the next one. Oh, wait . . . that's us. Nice guys shouldn't brag. But can we still go to Oslo?

- 2 cups (9 ounces) small ice cubes
- 2 ounces vodka
- 2 ounces dulce de leche, store-bought or homemade (see below)
- ½ ounce brandy
- ½ ounce vanilla liqueur
- ⅛ teaspoon salt
- 2 tablespoons light cream

Place the ice cubes, vodka, dulce de leche, brandy, vanilla liqueur, and salt in a large blender in that order. Cover and blend until smooth and caramel-colored, stopping the machine as necessary to shake down the canister, less than 1 minute.

Pour 1 tablespoon cream into each of two white wine glasses. Divide the drink between the two glasses.

makes two 8-ounce drinks

 To make Dulce de Leche, combine 4 cups whole milk, 1½ cups sugar, and ½ teaspoon baking soda in a large saucepan. Stir over medium heat until bubbling. Reduce the heat to low and cook at the barest simmer, stirring occasionally, for 1 hour. Add 2 teaspoons vanilla extract and cook at that bare simmer, stirring more often, until reduced to about 1½ cups, 1½ to 2 additional hours. As the sauce gets darker, stir more frequently—and never let it come to even a moderate simmer. Cool for at least 15 minutes, then pour and spoon into a large glass jar, seal, and refrigerate for up to 1 month.

FROZEN ROOTS

Consider this the finest root beer float you'll ever have. It'll remind you of your childhood. If you were the child of David Hasselhoff during the YouTube years.

- 2½ cups (11¼ ounces) small ice cubes
- 2½ ounces vodka
- 2 ounces root beer syrup (do not use carbonated root beer)
- 1 ounce root beer schnapps
- 2 ounces light cream

Put all the ingredients in a large blender in the order listed. Cover and blend until slushy and thick, stopping the machine as necessary to shake down the canister, less than 1 minute. Divide between two float or highball glasses.

makes two 9-ounce drinks

LIKE A PRO For a touch of sophistication, substitute Art in the Age Root liqueur for the root beer schnapps.

> **NIBBLE** Have some Maple Bacon Popcorn on the side. Toss popped popcorn with crumbled, cooked bacon plus some of its drippings, as well as a drizzle of maple syrup and a little ground black pepper in a large bowl. Spread onto a rimmed baking sheet and bake in a 350°F oven for 10 minutes. Transfer to a clean bowl to serve.

GARNISH
Stick a
Pirouette
cookie in
each glass.

FROZEN ORANGE BISCOTTI

To make this creamy frozen potation, you'll need fiori di Sicilia, a lauded baking flavoring. It's a fragrant mix of orange, vanilla, and floral notes. And you'll want to keep the bottle around for baking. Try a couple of drops in vanilla buttercream. Voilà: an Italian ice cream cake.

- 2 cups (9 ounces) small ice cubes
- ¾ cup orange sherbet
- 3 ounces vodka
- 3 ounces fresh orange juice
- 1 ounce triple sec
- 1 ounce caramel syrup (not caramel sauce), store-bought or homemade (page 26)
- ½ ounce Galliano
- Up to ⅛ teaspoon fiori di Sicilia

Add all the ingredients to a large blender in the order listed. Cover and blend until smooth and pale orange, stopping the machine as necessary to shake down the canister, less than 1 minute. Divide between two white wine glasses.

makes two 10-ounce drinks

HIGH-PROOF CHERRY PIE

The almost best cherry pie is made with a dash of almond extract. The really, really close to best cherry pie is made with almond extract and has a scoop of vanilla ice cream on the side. And the best cherry pie is all of the above plus booze. You could scrape it all into a blender or you could make our cocktail adaptation.

- 1½ cups (6¾ ounces) small ice cubes
- ¾ cup premium vanilla ice cream or gelato
- 8 pitted and stemmed red maraschino cherries (page 97)
- 2 ounces vodka
- 1 ounce cherry liqueur
- 1 ounce amaretto

Put all the ingredients in a large blender in the order listed. Cover and blend until smooth and rich, stopping the machine as necessary to make sure everything is well blended, less than 1 minute. Divide between two old-fashioned glasses.

makes two 9-ounce drinks

GARNISH Break a Hostess cherry hand pie in half and set a piece on the rim of each glass.

DIY EXCESS Tired of the lurid red? Here's how to make your own Maraschino Cherries. Mix 2 cups unsweetened pomegranate juice, 1 cup sugar, 3 tablespoons lemon juice, 2 star anise pods, 10 whole cloves, 3 allspice berries, and ¼ teaspoon salt in a large saucepan. Stir over medium-high heat until the sugar has dissolved, then bring to a low boil. Add 1 pound stemmed sweet cherries and ½ teaspoon almond extract. Bring back to a boil, stirring occasionally; then reduce the heat to low and simmer slowly, until the cherries have softened but not broken, 3 to 5 minutes. Remove from the heat and cool to room temperature. Pour into a large glass jar, seal, and refrigerate for up to 6 months.

NIBBLE Make Salt-and-Vinegar Potato Rounds for a quick snack. Cut medium-sized Yukon Gold potatoes into ¼-inch-thick slices. Toss in a large bowl with a generous amount of olive oil and a little ground black pepper. Arrange in a single layer on a large lipped baking sheet and bake in a 425°F oven for 30 minutes, until golden brown. Turn each slice over and continue baking until lightly browned on the other side, 12 to 18 minutes. Transfer the baking sheet with the potatoes to a wire rack, sprinkle with malt vinegar and coarse sea salt, and cool for a few minutes before serving.

TAILGATE

When the asphalt gets hot, real fans make frozen drinks—particularly classics with the right balance of flavors that get a casual, easy vibe going before the game.

Whenever you're cranking out frozen drinks at a tailgate party, use the ice cubes from the center of the cooler. The buried ones will give the drink the smoothest texture.

And if you're tailgating at your coffee table in front of the TV, keep the air-conditioning to a dull roar so these frozen wonders can cool you from the inside out.

Most of these are made to go with food: bratwursts, nachos, or burgers. While these flavors aren't quite as nuanced as others in this book, watch out: What they lack in complexity, they make up for in alcohol content (the better to knock your inhibitions down a notch so you can really support the team). Take timeouts—especially in the heat—and drink lots of water (for no added calories). You'll soon be ready for another round. Wait, who's playing?

THE PERFECT FROZEN MARGARITA

Getting the right ratio in any frozen drink is most of the work. This one's simple. It's equal parts of tequila, bitter orange liqueur, and lime juice. That's right: *equal parts*. Use less tequila than you think. You're not on spring break in Cancun; you're crafting a cocktail, even if it's on your tailgate. By adding a bitter orange hit to the mix—don't even consider triple sec—we balance those other flavors and turn the drink into an easy, smooth quaff.

> 4 cups (18 ounces) small ice cubes
> 3 ounces silver tequila
> 3 ounces bitter orange liqueur
> 3 ounces fresh lime juice
> 2 ounces simple syrup, store-bought or homemade
>   (page 25)

Put all the ingredients in a large blender in the order listed. Cover and blend until luxuriously slushy and very pale green, stopping the machine as necessary to shake down the canister, less than 1 minute. Divide between two large glasses.

makes two 16-ounce drinks

LIKE A PRO Use Key lime juice.

GARNISH
Coat the rim of the glass in a fine dusting of salt. Add a gummy worm, if desired.

FROZEN RASPBERRY MARGARITA

If you want to keep it real, you've gotta get seedy. Even though there are seeds aplenty in this drink, frozen raspberries will give it a thick, rich texture, impossible to mimic with raspberry purees or raspberry-flavored liqueurs. And that's not to mention their essence-of-summer flavor: tart, sweet, even slightly herbaceous. Listen, that's reason enough to get seedy.

1½ cups (6¾ ounces) small ice cubes
1 cup frozen raspberries
3 ounces silver tequila
1½ ounces simple syrup, store-bought or homemade (page 25)
1 ounce triple sec
1 ounce fresh lime juice
½ ounce raspberry liqueur

Put all the ingredients in a large blender in the order listed. Cover and blend until vampiric red and wonderfully thick, stopping the machine as necessary to shake down the canister, less than 1 minute. Pour into two ice-cold margarita glasses.

makes two 10-ounce drinks

GARNISH Use the channel knife (that is, the round eye) on a traditional citrus zester to create spirals of lime zest for the rim of each glass.

FROZEN MANGO MARGARITA

They say a perfectly ripe, juicy mango should be enjoyed naked and in a bathtub. While you can certainly drink this sweet and perfumy cocktail at a tailgate party, you could also hold to that mango advice. In fact, there's enough here for two. Invite your special someone to DVR the game and join you.

- 1 cup frozen mango cubes
- 2 cups (9 ounces) small ice cubes
- 3 ounces silver tequila
- 2 ounces triple sec
- 1½ ounces simple syrup, store-bought or homemade (page 25)
- 1½ ounces fresh lime juice

Put all the ingredients in a large blender in the order listed. Cover and blend until slushy-mushy and melony orange, stopping the machine as necessary to shake down the canister, less than 1 minute. Divide between two large glasses.

makes two 12-ounce drinks

GARNISH
Hang plastic monkeys off each glass.

LIKE A PRO Put ½ ounce grenadine (for homemade, see page 37) in each glass before you add the frozen drink.

NIBBLE For a colorful flare, have some Green Nachos on the side. Spread corn tortilla chips on a large rimmed baking sheet. Top with shredded Monterey Jack, sliced almonds, and jarred salsa verde. Broil 4 to 6 inches from the broiler element until the cheese melts and browns a bit, 2 to 3 minutes.

CHERRY LIME RICKEY-RITA

Back in the day, a cherry lime rickey was a soda fountain favorite: cherry syrup and lime soda over ice (jacked with gin in the best joints). We've done a mash-up of that drink with the Tex-Mex classic: dumped the gin for tequila, used fresh lime juice, and added sour cherry juice concentrate, available at most high-end supermarkets or countless online outlets. The combos are ridiculously sweet and tart; the result, the perfect antidote to the heat.

- 3 cups (13½ ounces) small ice cubes
- 3 ounces silver tequila
- 2½ ounces fresh lime juice
- 1½ ounces bitter orange liqueur
- 1 ounce simple syrup, store-bought or homemade (page 25)
- 1 ounce maraschino liqueur
- ½ ounce sour cherry juice concentrate (not sour cherry juice)

Put all the ingredients in a large blender in the order listed. Cover and blend until frosty pink and thick, stopping the machine as necessary to shake down the canister, less than 1 minute. Pour into two large glasses—or better yet, large clear plastic cups for that tailgating feel.

makes two 12-ounce drinks

NIBBLE Make Smoky Black Bean Dip for pita chips. Place all this in a food processor: drained and rinsed canned black beans, chopped red bell pepper, a little seeded canned chipotle chile in adobo sauce, a little olive oil, about the same amount of red wine vinegar, a little finely grated orange zest, and some ground cumin and salt for seasoning. Process until smooth and creamy. Scrape into a small bowl to serve.

THE PERFECT FROZEN DAIQUIRI

To craft the ultimate frozen daiquiri, we've pumped up the amount of rum to make sure the drink has a smooth but very real kick. Then we've given the whole thing a sweet accent with a splash of triple sec. Just remember: No amount of lime juice and sugar syrup can cover the taste of cheap rum. Use a good-quality bottling to make these drinks mellow and refreshing. They're dangerously easy to drink, so pace yourself.

- 3 cups (13½ ounces) small ice cubes
- 4 ounces silver rum
- 2½ ounces fresh lime juice
- 2 ounces simple syrup, store-bought or homemade (page 25)
- 1 ounce triple sec

Put all the ingredients in a large blender in the order listed. Cover and blend until slushy-smooth and pale white, stopping the machine as necessary to shake the canister, less than 1 minute. Divide between two large margarita glasses.

makes two 12-ounce drinks

LIKE A PRO Use Key lime juice.

GARNISH
Stick a lime
wedge on
the rim.

FROZEN STRAWBERRY DAIQUIRI

Welcome to brain freeze central, the intersection of ice cubes and frozen berries. It's hot out, the drink's super icy, and you want to down it. Take it easy. There's no need to rush. Besides, why not delay brain pain until the first fumble?

- 1 cup (4½ ounces) small ice cubes
- 1 cup frozen hulled strawberries
- 2 ounces silver rum
- 2 ounces aged rum
- 2 ounces thawed frozen limeade concentrate
- 1 ounce strawberry syrup
- ½ ounce fresh lime juice

Put all the ingredients in a large blender in the order listed. Cover and blend until bright red and thick, stopping the machine as necessary to shake down the canister, less than 1 minute. Divide between two tall glasses.

makes two 10-ounce drinks

GARNISH Stick a hulled fresh strawberry on each rim.

> **NIBBLE** It's easy to make Fried Artichoke Hearts for a snack. Thaw packages of frozen artichoke heart quarters, then gently squeeze the artichokes over the sink to remove excess moisture. Toss with flour until evenly coated, then drop into a pot of 350°F canola or vegetable oil and fry until crisp, flipping occasionally. Use a slotted spoon to transfer to a plate lined with paper towels. Sprinkle with salt while hot.

FROZEN BLACKBERRY ELDERFLOWER DAIQUIRI

Don't freeze those blackberries—or even use thawed, frozen blackberries. You want the intense, slightly sour pop of the fresh fruit to give this twisted classic supreme flavor. The elderflower liqueur gives the drink a decidedly summery—and floral—note that keeps all those berries in check.

- 2½ cups (11¼ ounces) small ice cubes
- ¼ cup fresh blackberries
- 2½ ounces vodka
- 2 ounces blackberry syrup (not liqueur)
- 1 ounce elderflower liqueur
- 1 ounce sweetened lime juice, store-bought or homemade (page 41)
- ½ ounce fresh lime juice

Put all the ingredients in a large blender in the order listed. Cover and blend until slushy, stopping the machine as necessary to shake down the canister, less than 1 minute. Pour into two tall glasses.

GARNISH
Skewer blackberries to dip in the drinks.

makes two 10-ounce drinks

PINK COLADA

You can get rid of those spring break embarrassments by skipping the colada mix and rotgut rum. You're an adult now. Go for the real deal: two kinds of rum, fresh pineapple (rather than sweetened pineapple juice), unsweetened coconut milk (for a purer flavor), and caramel syrup for a little depth. We've turned it pink with grenadine, a sweet-tart touch to balance the surprisingly complex flavors.

- 2 cups cubed, peeled pineapple (about ⅓ medium pineapple)
- 2 cups (9 ounces) small ice cubes
- 2 ounces aged rum
- 2 ounces spiced rum (see below)
- 2 ounces regular or low-fat coconut milk
- 1 ounce caramel syrup (not caramel sauce), store-bought or homemade (page 26)
- 1 ounce grenadine, store-bought or homemade (page 37)

Put all the ingredients in a large blender in the order listed. Cover and blend until creamy smooth and pale pink, stopping the machine as necessary to shake down the canister, less than 1 minute. Divide between two tall glasses.

makes two 14-ounce drinks

GARNISH Go with a pineapple wedge and maraschino cherry on a skewer.

Make your own Spiced Rum. Buy a bottle of gold rum, open it, and pour out (or use up) 2 to 3 ounces. Add to the bottle a split-lengthwise vanilla bean, a 4-inch cinnamon stick, up to a half of a star anise pod, 4 whole cloves, 3 allspice berries, and two strips of zest from an orange. Seal again and set aside for anywhere between 3 days and 3 months. The longer it sits, the more potent the infusion will become.

FROZEN KEY LIME PIE

Key limes have a bright, intense sourness, more so than standard Persian limes. There are also tons of seeds in each Key lime, so you'll need to juice them over a small strainer or fine-mesh sieve. Here, we've used a little gingerbread liqueur to mimic the graham cracker crust in many versions of the classic dessert. Call it a very easy way to get your pie fix.

- 2 cups (9 ounces) small ice cubes
- 2½ ounces regular or low-fat sweetened condensed milk
- 2 ounces vodka
- 1½ ounces fresh Key lime juice
- 1 ounce gingerbread liqueur (not ginger liqueur)

Put all the ingredients in a large blender in the order listed. Cover and blend until thick and slushy, stopping the machine as necessary to shake down the canister, less than 1 minute. Divide between two large glasses.

makes two 8-ounce drinks

GARNISH

Serve with gingersnap cookies on the side.

CHERRY ITALIAN ICE

No more sweating on the concrete! Here's what a cherry popsicle wants to be when it grows up. This drink mimics the classic flavors of Italian ices with a slushy, rich texture. But skip those little paper cups and tiny spoons that always come with Italian ices. You'll want a clear glass for the color and an iced-tea spoon to get every drop.

- 2½ cups (11¼ ounces) small ice cubes
- 2½ ounces vodka
- 2½ ounces sweet cherry syrup (not *sour* cherry syrup)
- 1 ounce maraschino liqueur
- 1 ounce fresh lemon juice

Put all the ingredients in a large blender in the order listed. Cover and blend until slushy thick and bright red, stopping the machine as necessary to shake down the canister, less than 1 minute. Divide the drink between two small glasses.

makes two 9-ounce drinks

LIKE A PRO If you've made your own maraschino cherries (see page 97), use the strained liquor right out of the jar.

NIBBLE Slice up a Garlic and Rosemary Focaccia. Buy unbaked pizza dough and press it on an oiled baking sheet into a rustic circle, about ½ inch thick. Sprinkle with chopped, pitted black olives, minced garlic, minced tinned anchovy fillets, and chopped rosemary leaves. Drizzle generously with olive oil and bake in a 400°F oven until firm and brown, 12 to 15 minutes. Cool on the baking sheet for 5 minutes before slicing into wedges. Or cool and store uncovered at room temperature for up to 3 hours.

CHILLY CHERRY LIBRE

Cuba Libres may be the easiest drink of the summer: cola, rum, and lime wedges. But there's always room for improvement. We've used cherry pop and morphed the whole thing into a blender drink, perfect with bratwurst or chicken off the grate. You'll need to freeze the cola in advance and make more ice cubes than you think you'll need. Everyone will want in on this play.

> 1⅓ cups plus ¼ cup cherry cola
> 3 ounces aged rum
> 1 tablespoon lime syrup (not juice or concentrate)

Pour 1⅓ cups cherry cola into a glass. Use a fork to stir vigorously until flat so the cubes will form more evenly. Pour into ice cube trays and freeze for 12 hours or up to 3 weeks.

Place the cola ice cubes, rum, and the remaining ¼ cup cherry cola in a large blender in that order. Cover and blend until smooth, less than 1 minute.

Divide the lime syrup between two clear plastic cups. Pour the drink on top as the syrup swirls up the sides.

makes two 7-ounce drinks

GARNISH
Have lime
wedges at
the ready.

LIKE A PRO Use traditional cola (rather than cherry cola) and add 8 dashes cherry bitters to the blender.

NIBBLE To make a Chunky Black Bean Salsa, mix one 15-ounce can drained and rinsed black beans, one 4½-ounce can chopped hot or mild green chiles, 1 chopped plum tomato, ¼ cup corn kernels, ¼ cup chopped red onion, ¼ cup minced cilantro leaves, 1 tablespoon fresh lime juice, and ½ teaspoon ground cumin in a serving bowl. Serve with corn tortilla chips.

BOURBON MINT SLUSH

If you're ever tailgating at the Kentucky Derby (you never know), you'll need this frozen concoction to ward off the late spring heat. Or just stay home, invite your friends over, and put the Derby on the TV. Or skip the TV, dress your friends up in horse outfits, and have them run up and down the hallway. After a couple of rounds, you won't notice the difference.

- 3 cups (13½ ounces) small ice cubes
- 6 fresh mint leaves
- 4 ounces bourbon
- 2 ounces fresh lemon juice
- 2 ounces simple syrup, store-bought or homemade (page 25)

Put all the ingredients in a large blender in the order listed. Cover and blend until slushy and thick, stopping the machine as necessary to shake down the canister, less than 1 minute. Pour into two short glasses (or maybe even Jefferson cups).

makes two 10-ounce drinks

GARNISH Thread mint leaves along each glass or serve with decorative straws.

SLUSHY WHITE SANGRIA

Sangria in a blender? Generalissimo Francisco Franco would have had your head. But then again, he had everybody's head. Anyway, just crank up the blender and try it. The orange and peach flavors are balanced by the little bit of lemon juice, a bright bit of spark in each glass. ¡*Salud!*

- 2 cups frozen peach slices
- 1 cup (4½ ounces) small ice cubes
- 1¼ cups chilled fruit-forward white wine, such as Riesling
- 3 ounces fresh orange juice
- 2 ounces simple syrup, store-bought or homemade (page 25)
- 1 ounce peach liqueur
- 1 ounce triple sec
- ½ ounce fresh lemon juice

Put all the ingredients in a large blender in the order listed. Cover and blend until slushy thick and pale yellow, stopping the machine as necessary to shake down the canister, less than 1 minute. Pour into two large red wine glasses, preferably stemless wine glasses.

makes two 14-ounce drinks

NIBBLE Chow down on some Chorizo-Cheese Skewers. Slice dried, Spanish chorizo links into ½-inch sections and cook in a skillet set over medium-high heat until crisp, turning often, 3 to 4 minutes. Cool a few minutes, then thread the pieces of chorizo onto skewers between cubes of Manchego cheese.

THE FROZEN LEMONADE BLUES

Like a good country-western song, you never know which way a blue drink is gonna go. Is it raspberry, orange, banana, or even bubblegum flavor? This time, it's lemon with a hint of vanilla. Surprise!

- 2½ cups (11¼ ounces) small ice cubes
- 2 ounces vodka
- 1½ ounces thawed frozen lemonade concentrate
- 1 ounce vanilla liqueur
- 1 ounce blue Curaçao

Put all the ingredients in a large blender in the order listed. Cover and blend until icy and grainy-smooth, stopping the machine as necessary to shake down the canister, less than 1 minute. Divide the drink between two Mason jars.

makes two 8-ounce drinks

PUNCH
IN THE FACE

It's fall. You should be apple picking. Or blackberry picking. Instead, you're tailgating. But that doesn't mean you can't enjoy the fruits of the harvest. Apples are fruits. Blackberries are fruits. Limes are fruits. Vodka's a fruit. Whatever, there'll still be apples on the trees after the Super Bowl in February, right? Right?

- 2 cups (9 ounces) small ice cubes
- 2 ounces thawed frozen unsweetened apple juice
     concentrate
- 1½ ounces vodka
- 1½ ounces blackberry-flavored brandy
- 1 ounce triple sec
- ½ ounce sweetened lime juice, store-bought or homemade
     (page 41)

Put all the ingredients in a large blender in the order listed. Cover and blend until creamy-icy and pale purple, stopping the machine as necessary to shake down the canister, less than 1 minute. Divide between two short glasses.

makes two 9-ounce drinks

NIBBLE Serve up a batch of Buffalo Shrimp. Mix equal parts bottled hot red sauce (like Frank's RedHot) and melted butter with a generous splash of white vinegar, a little Worcestershire sauce, a pinch of sugar, and a very small pinch of garlic powder. Stir in a saucepan set over medium heat until hot, then use it as a barbecue mop on shell-on, deveined, large shrimp as they grill directly over the heat. Get ready to get messy. For a creamy dip, mix equal parts sour cream, mayonnaise, and crumbled blue cheese with a little lemon juice and buttermilk in a bowl. Season with lots of ground black pepper.

FROZEN SLAMMER

Y'all need the South in yer mouth to enjoy 'ar frozen version of an Alabama Slammer, which is Dixie's version of Long Island Iced Tea. Both have just enough fruit juice to mellow the vat of alcohol in each glass. You'll soon have no trouble with that accent.

- 3 cups (13½ ounces) small ice cubes
- 2 ounces bourbon
- 1 ounce Southern Comfort
- 1 ounce sloe gin
- 1 ounce amaretto
- 1 ounce fresh lemon juice
- 1 ounce thawed frozen orange juice concentrate
- 1 ounce simple syrup, store-bought or homemade (page 25)

Put all the ingredients in a large blender in the order listed. Cover and blend until a rosy salmon-colored slush, stopping the machine as necessary to shake down the canister, less than 1 minute. Pour into two large glasses.

makes two 14-ounce drinks

LIKE A PRO Use a peach liqueur like Mathilde Pêche instead of Southern Comfort.

GARNISH
Serve with a small glass of water and two aspirin.

ACKNOWLEDGMENTS

It takes a party to make a book. If only we'd served more drinks! Our deep gratitude to:

- Aaron Wehner, our publisher
- Doris Cooper, our associate publisher
- Emma Brodie, our editor
- Kate Slate (again!), our copyeditor
- Pam Krauss (again and again!), our champion
- Susan Ginsburg (again and again and again!), our agent
- Stacy Testa, our source for all answers
- Ashley Tucker, the book's designer
- Jane Treuhaft and Michael Nagin, its art directors
- Natasha Martin, its PR director
- Kevin Sweeting, its marketing director
- Evan Sung, its (consummate) photographer
- Kira Corbin, its (stylish) prop stylist
- Jan and Jerry Rathbun, our dogwalkers
- and Karen O'Dell, our kitchen help

And many thanks to these people whose products made the party happen:

- Reagan Nickl at Blendtech
- Mary Rodgers and Ilona Gollinger at Waring
- Laura Pegg at Falls Communication for VitaMix
- Marybeth Brault at Hamilton-Beach
- Emily Forrest at OXO
- Deborah Marskey at Shrub & Co.
- Suzanne Geel at Monin
- and Andrea Ramirez at Torani

INDEX